First World War
and Army of Occupation
War Diary
France, Belgium and Germany

59 DIVISION
176 Infantry Brigade
South Staffordshire Regiment
2/5th (T.F.) Battalion
25 February 1917 - 31 January 1918

WO95/3021/7

The Naval & Military Press Ltd
www.nmarchive.com
Published in association with The National Archives

Published by

The Naval & Military Press Ltd

Unit 10 Ridgewood Industrial Park,

Uckfield, East Sussex,

TN22 5QE England

Tel: +44 (0) 1825 749494

www.naval-military-press.com

www.nmarchive.com

This diary has been reprinted in facsimile from the original. Any imperfections are inevitably reproduced and the quality may fall short of modern type and cartographic standards.

© **Crown Copyright**
Images reproduced by permission of The National Archives, London, England, 2015.

Contents

Document type	Place/Title	Date From	Date To
Heading	WO95/3021/7		
Heading	59th Division 176th Infy Bde 2-5th South Staffs Regt Feb 1917-1918 Jan		
War Diary	Codford	25/02/1917	25/02/1917
War Diary	Southampton	25/02/1917	25/02/1917
War Diary	Harve	26/02/1917	26/02/1917
War Diary	Soleaux	27/02/1917	27/02/1917
War Diary	Saint Fuschin	28/02/1917	28/02/1917
Heading	War Diary of 2/5th South Staffs Regt From 1st March 1917 To 30th March 1917 Vol II		
War Diary	Fouilloy	01/03/1917	01/03/1917
War Diary	Mericourt	02/03/1917	07/03/1917
War Diary	Foucacourt	08/03/1917	08/03/1917
War Diary	Berny	09/03/1917	15/03/1917
War Diary	Foncacourt	16/03/1917	21/03/1917
War Diary	Cizancourt	22/03/1917	25/03/1917
War Diary	Briost	26/03/1917	26/03/1917
War Diary	Brie	28/03/1917	30/03/1917
Heading	War Diary of 2/5th South Staffs Regiment From 1st April 1917 To 30th April 1917 Vol 3		
War Diary	Brie	01/04/1917	02/04/1917
War Diary	Mons-En Chaussee	03/04/1917	03/04/1917
War Diary	Vraignes	06/04/1917	06/04/1917
War Diary	Bernes	08/04/1917	10/04/1917
War Diary	Le Verguier	11/04/1917	27/04/1917
War Diary	Jeancourt	30/04/1917	30/04/1917
Heading	War Diary of 2/5th South Stafford Regiment From 2nd May 1917 To 31st May 1917 Vol 4		
War Diary	Vraignes	02/05/1917	06/05/1917
War Diary	Hervilly	08/05/1917	11/05/1917
War Diary	Trenches	13/05/1917	15/05/1917
War Diary	Hervilly	20/05/1917	20/05/1917
War Diary	Trenches	21/05/1917	23/05/1917
War Diary	Hervilly	24/05/1917	31/05/1917
Heading	War Diary of 2/5th South Stafford Regiment From 1st June 1917 To 30th June 1917 Vol 5		
War Diary	Equancourt	01/06/1917	11/06/1917
War Diary	Metz-en-Couture	14/06/1917	18/06/1917
War Diary	Beaucamp	22/06/1917	30/06/1917
Heading	War Diary of 2/5th South Stafford Regiment From 1st July 1917 To 31st July 1917 Vol 6		
War Diary	Beaucamp	01/07/1917	01/07/1917
War Diary	Equancourt	02/07/1917	06/07/1917
War Diary	Barastre	07/07/1917	20/07/1917
Heading	War Diary of 2/5th Bn South Staffordshire Regiment From 1st August 1917 To 31st August 1917 Vol 7		
War Diary	Barastre	24/08/1917	24/08/1917
War Diary	Bouzincourt	31/08/1917	31/08/1917
Operation(al) Order(s)	2/5th Bn. South Staffordshire Regiment Operation Order No.30	22/08/1917	22/08/1917

Miscellaneous	2/5th Bn South Staffordshire Regiment Instructions No.1 issued in conjunction with Operation Orders No. 30	22/08/1917	22/08/1917
Miscellaneous	2/5th Bn South Staffordshire Regiment Administrative Instructions No.1	27/08/1917	27/08/1917
Miscellaneous	2/5th Bn South Staffordshire Regiment Battalion Circular No.1	27/08/1917	27/08/1917
Miscellaneous	2/5th Bn South Staffordshire Regiment Administrative Instructions No.2	29/08/1917	29/08/1917
Miscellaneous	2/5th South Stafford Regiment Marche Entrain Table		
Operation(al) Order(s)	2/5th Bn. South Staffordshire Regiment Operation Order No.33	29/08/1917	29/08/1917
Heading	War Diary of 2/5th Bn. South Stafford Regiment From 1st Sept 1917 To 30th Sept 1917 Vol 8		
War Diary	Winnezeele	01/09/1917	19/09/1917
War Diary	Brandhoek	19/09/1917	21/09/1917
War Diary	Goldfish Chateau	21/09/1917	22/09/1917
War Diary	Bank Farm	23/09/1917	24/09/1917
War Diary	Goldfish Chateau	25/09/1917	25/09/1917
War Diary	Pommern Castle	26/09/1917	26/09/1917
War Diary	Shell Hole East of Primrose-Cottage	26/09/1917	27/09/1917
War Diary	Wieltje Dugout	28/09/1917	28/09/1917
War Diary	Vlamertinghe	29/09/1917	29/09/1917
War Diary	Watou	30/09/1917	30/09/1917
Miscellaneous	2/5th Bn South Staffordshire Regiment Administrative Instructions No.3	29/08/1917	29/08/1917
Heading	War Diary of 2/5th South Staffs Regiment From 1st Oct 1917 To 31st Oct 1917 Vol 9		
War Diary	Watou	01/10/1917	01/10/1917
War Diary	Guarbecque	02/10/1917	07/10/1917
War Diary	Lisbourg	09/10/1917	10/10/1917
War Diary	Sains-En-Gohelle	11/10/1917	12/10/1917
War Diary	Leivin	13/10/1917	15/10/1917
War Diary	Cite De Riaumont	16/10/1917	21/10/1917
War Diary	Cite-De Roullincourt	22/10/1917	30/10/1917
Heading	War Diary of 2/5th South Staffs Regiment From 1st Nov 1917 To 30th Nov 1917 Vol 10		
War Diary	Vancouver Camp	01/11/1917	01/11/1917
War Diary	Chateau De La Haie	01/11/1917	01/11/1917
War Diary	Vancouver Camp	05/11/1917	07/11/1917
War Diary	Avion Sector	08/11/1917	14/11/1917
War Diary	Red Trench	15/11/1917	17/11/1917
War Diary	Alberta Camp Souchez Vimy 36c S.W.3 S 13 B 18.86	17/11/1917	17/11/1917
War Diary	Vancouver Camp Chateau-De-La-Haie Sheet 36 B W 12a 30.45	18/11/1917	18/11/1917
War Diary	Grand Servins Sheet 36 B Q 34 b 5.7	19/11/1917	19/11/1917
War Diary	Carency	19/11/1917	19/11/1917
War Diary	Berneville	19/11/1917	21/11/1917
War Diary	Courcelles Le Comte	23/11/1917	23/11/1917
War Diary	Railton Camp	27/11/1917	27/11/1917
War Diary	Ribecourt	27/11/1917	29/11/1917
War Diary	Fontaine Notre Dame Sector	29/11/1917	30/11/1917
Heading	War Diary of 2/5th South Staffs Regiment From 1st Dec 1917 To 31st Dec 1917 Vol 11		
War Diary	Fontaine Notre Dame Sector	01/12/1917	05/12/1917
War Diary	Havrincourt Wood	05/12/1917	05/12/1917

War Diary	Lechelle	06/12/1917	10/12/1917
War Diary	Flesquieres	12/12/1917	18/12/1917
War Diary	Old British Front Line	20/12/1917	20/12/1917
War Diary	Barastre	24/12/1917	25/12/1917
Heading	War Diary of 2/5th Bn. South Staffs Regiment From 1st Jan 1918 To 31st Jan 1918 Vol 12		
War Diary	Manin	01/01/1918	31/01/1918

3005/3021/7

59TH DIVISION
176TH INFY BDE

2-5TH SOUTH STAFFS REGT.

FEB 1917 - ~~JLY 1918~~ 1918 JAN

(also 1916 JAN and FEB)

(DISBANDED JAN 18)

2/5. BN. S. STAFF REG.

Jly - 1918

Original

WAR DIARY
or
INTELLIGENCE SUMMARY.

Army Form C. 2118.

(Erase heading not required.)

Instructions regarding War Diaries and Intelligence Summaries are contained in F. S. Regs., Part II. and the Staff Manual respectively. Title pages will be prepared in manuscript.

2/5 S/R 2/5/176/59 Vol I

Place	Date	Hour	Summary of Events and Information	Remarks and references to Appendices
Bedford	25/7/17	6.53am	B Coy D Coys left Bedford Strength 19 Officers 575 other Ranks. Arrived Southampton 2.15 AM	
"	"	7am	" " " 6 " " 93 " " "	10 & 2 pm
Southampton	25/7/17		Battalion left Southampton on S.S. Queen Alexandra & S.S. Harvé	
Harvé	26/7/17	1 AM	Battalion arrive at Harvé docks. Disembarking at about 8 AM. Proceeding to No. 5 Rest Camp	
			Left rest camp at noon to entrain at Rouleaux at 6.15 to point adjacent Mid: at 10 p.m	
Solesmes	27/7/17	6 am	Train arrived and Battalion proceeded by route march to Goint Junction and billeted for night. Major Stewart Morley & Capt McAlister Smith Arthur & Elliott and Baites went forward to Battalion.	
Goint Junction	28/7/17	9 am	Battalion marched to Landroy distance about 18 miles, arriving about 11 pm. Some Billets too far for the night. Men harassed dull hot contending Bombin & wet about 20 men fell out.	S.1

Stewart Morley major
2/5 Yk Spath Nyft Regt

Army Form C. 2118.

WAR DIARY
or
INTELLIGENCE SUMMARY
(Erase heading not required.)

Original

Vol II

Confidential

War Diary
of
2/5th South Staffs. Regt
from 1st March 1917
To 30th March 1917

Place	Date	Hour	Summary of Events and Information	Remarks and references to Appendices

Army Form C. 2118.

WAR DIARY

INTELLIGENCE SUMMARY

(Erase heading not required.)

9/5 - 8 Staffs Regt

Instructions regarding War Diaries and Intelligence Summaries are contained in F. S. Regs., Part II. and the Staff Manual respectively. Title Pages will be prepared in manuscript.

Place	Date	Hour	Summary of Events and Information	Remarks and references to Appendices
Louilley	1/7	9am	Batt. Route marched to Mericourt via Hamel, being thereout distance about 12 miles, arriving about 2pm as men fell out.	
Mericourt	2/7		Battalion remained in Rest Camp. A & B Coys in Battle Of Div Hd.Qrs. Camp	
Mericourt	3/7		Battalion remained in Rest Camp. 5 Officers 9/10th other Ranks joined from 107th Brigade dismtd Coy & 2 other officers & 9 OR seconded to join 153rd Brigade to Light Bane Bombs FA.	
Mericourt	4/7		Battalion remained in Rest Camp	
Mericourt	5/7		Battalion remained in Rest Camp	
Mericourt	6/7		Battalion remained in Rest Camp	
Mericourt	7/7	1pm	Battalion remained in Rest Camp the Battalion marched to Touvencourt arriving about 4pm and billeted for the night	

WAR DIARY
INTELLIGENCE SUMMARY

(Erase heading not required.)

Army Form C. 2118.

Place	Date	Hour	Summary of Events and Information	Remarks and references to Appendices
Fouencourt	8/3/17	5pm	Battalion proceeded to relieve the 6th N. Staff. R. in support trenches at BERNY	
BERNY	9/3/17		Battalion remained in Support trenches	
BERNY	10/3/17		Battalion remained in Support trenches	
BERNY	11/3/17	6pm	Battalion relieved 6th N. Staffs Regt. in front line trenches which were shelled rather heavily. About 3 p.m. 9043 L/Cpl Hughes seriously wounded 9557 Sgt Davis killed	
	12/3/17		Battalion remained in Front line trenches. 9t Blanchard killed 1663 Pte Laurie wounded	
	13/3/17		Battalion remained in Front line. 2385 Pte Blanchard killed. 2712 L/Cpl Butler wounded. Pte Leplock 2740 Pte Anstone 9749 Pte Lambrick 9923 Pte Green 3149 Pte White	
	14/3/17		Battalion remained in Front line. 9t Th. wounded 2331 L/Cpl Tate 2772 Pte Brown 7 Pte H. Rollington 2692 L/Cpl Lavers 1664 Pte Worrall 2793 Sgt Stevens 291 Pte Boulton 2886 Pte Rollinson.	

WAR DIARY
INTELLIGENCE SUMMARY
(Erase heading not required.)

Army Form C. 2118.

Place	Date	Hour	Summary of Events and Information	Remarks and references to Appendices
Foucaucourt	15/4	6.30pm	Battalion was Relieved by 4/North Staff Regt and returned to rest camp Foucaucourt 457. 4th N Staffs Brigade 208 Bde. Hd Bruniers (see order)	
	16/4		Battalion remained at Rest Camp	
	17/4		Battalion remained at Rest Camp	
Foucaucourt	18/4	7 pm	Battalion proceeded to take up position vacated by 4th N Staffs Regt. owing to enemy retiring	
	19/4		Battalion advanced in support of Line Trenches	
	20/4		— do —	
	21/4		— do —	

Army Form C. 2118.

WAR DIARY
INTELLIGENCE SUMMARY
(Erase heading not required.)

9/5 S Staffs Regt.

Place	Date	Hour	Summary of Events and Information	Remarks and references to Appendices
Liencourt	22/3/17	6.30AM	Batt proceeded to relieve the 7th 2/6 Worly Regt 2/6/17	
Liencourt	23/3/17		Batt remained at Liencourt	
Liencourt	24/3/17		Do	
Liencourt	25/3/17	3PM	Battalion proceeded to Briast	
Briast	26/3/17		Battalion remained at Briast	
Briast	27/3/17	9AM	Battalion proceeded to Brie (Bridgehead)	
Brie	28/3/17		Battalion remained at Brie	Do
Brie	29/3/17		Do	Do
Brie	30/3/17		Do	Do

Lawrence Lt Colonel

Army Form C. 2118.

WAR DIARY
or
INTELLIGENCE SUMMARY.
(Erase heading not required.)

Instructions regarding War Diaries and Intelligence Summaries are contained in F. S. Regs., Part II. and the Staff Manual respectively. Title pages will be prepared in manuscript.

Hour, Date, Place	Summary of Events and Information	Remarks and references to Appendices

Vol 3

S.3

Confidential

Original

War Diary

of

2/5th South Staffs Regiment

From:- 1st April 1917.
To:- 30th April 1917

Army Form C. 2118.

WAR DIARY
or
INTELLIGENCE SUMMARY.
(Erase heading not required.)

Instructions regarding War Diaries and Intelligence Summaries are contained in F. S. Regs., Part II. and the Staff Manual respectively. Title pages will be prepared in manuscript.

Place	Date	Hour	Summary of Events and Information	Remarks and references to Appendices
Brie	1st		No 202513 Pr Barnard A. died in hospital of Syncope	
—	2nd		Battalion marched to Mons-en-Chaussée. Distance 22 miles. East men in tents	
Mons-en-Chaussée	3rd	6pm	Battalion marched to Vraignes. Men in billets	
Vraignes	6th	2.30am	Battalion marched via Hancourt to Beronés relieving 2/6th Notts + Derby Regt + taking over new posts. Nos 200868 Pr Sawry J. and 202305 Pr Tyler W. wounded in action	
Beronés	8th		Major J. Parkin 2/6 N. Staff Regt took over command of the Battalion during absence of Lt.Col J.A. Armatroy	
—	9th		No 201866 Pr Sentance wounded in action	
—	10th		Took over the trenches of 2/5 Notts + Derby Regt at Le Verguier	
Le Verguier	11th		Nos 262883 Pr Zelly E, 202891 Pr Rhodes H, and 200344 Pr Finch S wounded	
—	12th		No 202312 L/C Millotts J. was wounded and 202163 Pr Hill H. wounded	
			(staff windbrichs)	
—	13th		No 202910 Pr Lowrie J was wounded	
—	14th		Lt.Col J.A. Armatroy resumed command	

WAR DIARY
or
INTELLIGENCE SUMMARY.
(Erase heading not required.)

Army Form C. 2118.

Place	Date	Hour	Summary of Events and Information	Remarks and references to Appendices
Le Touquin	16th		Major J.t. Hughes 1/6th S. Staffs reported and took over duties of second in command.	
—	18th		Brig-Gen Humphreys handed over command of 176th Brigade to Brig-Gen R.A. Currie. No 202982 Pte Williment wounded (self inflicted)	
—	19th		Lieut Holden T.G. was wounded.	
—	21st		Battalion took over advanced line of trenches which has been partially dug by 2/5th N. Staffs. No 202146 Pte Greeno Alf killed	
—	22nd		2/Lieut Millin reported for duty from 5th (Res) Battalion. Nos 200690, Cpl Page A. 202156 Pte Moore J.W. 209943 Sgt Westwood J. 2218 Arm. St. Sgt Camfem H. 202773 Pte York H. Killed and Nos 202565 Pte Greenleaf N. and 202656 Pte Wynn A. were wounded.	
—	24th		Advanced our line 800 yards on a front of 200 yards. No 202762 Pte Morey B.T. died in hospital of Bronchitis.	
—	25th		No 202096 L/Cpl Westbury E. was killed and No 201069 Pte Carter J. Killed	
—	26th		2/Lieuts Roberts and Millen reported for duty from 3rd Battalion	

Army Form C. 2118.

WAR DIARY
or
INTELLIGENCE SUMMARY.
(Erase heading not required.)

Place	Date	Hour	Summary of Events and Information	Remarks and references to Appendices
Le Verguier	27th		Capt Booth a.b. 1/10 Monmouth Regt reports Battalion was relieved by 2/5th North Staffs Regt & marches to Jeancourt.	
Jeancourt	30th		Battalion was relieved by 2/4th Lincoln Regt and marches to Vraignes (in recerve)	

Armstrong Lieut-Col
Commdg 2/5th South Stafford Regt.

Army Form C. 2118.

WAR DIARY
or
INTELLIGENCE SUMMARY
(Erase heading not required.)

Vol 4

Confidential

War Diary
of
2/5th South Stafford Regiment

From:- 2nd May, 1917
To:- 31st May, 1917

Place	Date	Hour	Summary of Events and Information	Remarks and references to Appendices
Original				

WAR DIARY
INTELLIGENCE SUMMARY

Army Form C. 2118.

May

Place	Date	Hour	Summary of Events and Information	Remarks and references to Appendices
Maigues	2nd	3 PM	Inspection by Major General Romer, commanding 59th Division	
	6th	10 am	Battalion marched to HERVILLY & took over billets from 2/5th Sherwood Foresters. Battalion was in support. A Coy at HESBECOURT, an B.C.D at HERVILLY	
Hervilly	8th		No. 200906 Pte Jeff J (attached T.M.B) wounded. "A" Coy at HESBECOURT held in readiness to move at 15 mins notice to support front line.	
	11th	8 PM	Battalion relieved 2/5th North Staffs in Brigade Right Subsector. A & D Coys in Outpost line & B & C Coys in main line of Resistance	
	13th		No 9843 Pte Grosvenor J and 200946 Pte Shotliff BK wounded	
	14th		No 200311 Sgt Mitchell P slightly wounded	
	15th	9.30 pm	Battalion relieved by 2/5th North Staffs and marched back to HERVILLY (A&C Coys) and HESBECOURT (B Coy)	
Hervilly	20th	8.0 PM	Battalion relieved 2/5th North Staffs in Brigade Right Subsector. B&C Coys in outpost line and A&D Coys in main line of Resistance	
Trenches	21		No 200715 Pte Robertson J wounded	

WAR DIARY
or
INTELLIGENCE SUMMARY.

(Erase heading not required.)

Army Form C. 2118.

Place	Date	Hour	Summary of Events and Information	Remarks and references to Appendices
Irruthes	22		Capt J.B. Rich severely wounded	
—	23	9.30am	Battalion relieved by Cavalry troops. A + B Coys by 6th Cavalry and C+D Coys by 17th Lancers. Battalion marches to HERMIES (AB Coys) and HESBE COURT (C Coy)	
Hermily	24		C Coy marches to HERMIES, joining Battalion	
—	31st	5.30pm	Battalion marches to EQUANCOURT arriving at 9.30pm. Then in tents	

Army Form C. 2118.

WAR DIARY
or
INTELLIGENCE SUMMARY

(Erase heading not required.)

Vol 6

Confidential

War Diary
of
2/5th South Stafford Regiment

From 1st June 1917
To 30th June 1917

Original

Jollinshead Lieut Col
Comdg 2/5 South Stafford Regt

WAR DIARY or INTELLIGENCE SUMMARY

Army Form C. 2118.

Place	Date	Hour	Summary of Events and Information	Remarks and references to Appendices
Bouzencourt	9th		General Reserve	
	10th		In Camp at Equipment Inspection by Divisional Commander General C.B.B. White	
	11th		Major General Sinclair MacLagan Farewell Parade on Major General's departure	
			Attached to Reg en Corbie and relieved 26th Battalion	
Meg-en-Corbie	17th		2030 Cpl Allin J.B. C Coy wounded Rifle Grenade accident	
	17/18		The following casualties occurred during the night 17/18	
			7200 Pte Kearsby D - Shrapnel left arm slight	
			2020 Pte Thomas C - Gas	
			2023 Pte Simmonds R - Gas & wounds 17 & 8.1	
			3624 Pte Pullman E - Shrapnel wound scalp severe	
			2033 Pte Rosa E - Shrapnel Reg slight	
Beaucamp	22/23		Relieved 26th Batt Support Post in Bivouacs	
			On night 22/23 Ant. Sutin in front line front U.S. Post men of the wounded	
	25/26		2900 L/Cpl Lacon C - Killed	
			2022 L/Cpl EF Hall R.S.	
	26/27		2620 Pte Luciano F - Ruined Rifles	
			2031 Pte Phillips D - Accidental fall by L/Cpl Evans Geo	

Army Form C. 2118.

WAR DIARY
or
INTELLIGENCE SUMMARY.
(Erase heading not required.)

Instructions regarding War Diaries and Intelligence Summaries are contained in F. S. Regs., Part II. and the Staff Manual respectively. Title pages will be prepared in manuscript.

Place	Date	Hour	Summary of Events and Information	Remarks and references to Appendices
Beaucamp	29th		No 202459 Pte Boulhwood W Wounded left hand Machinegun Sight	OO
	30th		240140 Cpl Hawthorne J — — forearm Bullet Severe	OO
			Hawthorne J/ 1st Coy 1/5 South Stafford Regt	

A6(..) Wt W11422/M1160 350,000 12/ D. D. & L. Forms/C./2118/14.

Army Form C. 2118.

WAR DIARY
or
INTELLIGENCE SUMMARY
(Erase heading not required.)

Vol 6

Confidential

Min. Passed.   S.b

Original

War Diary
of
2/5th South Stafford Regiment

From:- 1st July 1917
To:- 31st July 1917

WAR DIARY
INTELLIGENCE SUMMARY

July 1917 — Page 1

Place	Date	Hour	Summary of Events and Information	Remarks and references to Appendices
Beaucamp	1st		The Battalion was relieved on the night of 1st/2nd July 1917 by the 2/4th Bn. Lincoln Regt in the Brigade Right Sub-Sector. Map Reference Sheet 57c SE. 1/20000 Q5 d 30 30 – Q 12 b 15 95. On completion of relief at about 12/45 A.M. the Battalion marched to EQUANCOURT V.16.b.6.1 Ref Sheet 57 c. S.E. 1/20000. The Battalion furnished 2 Officers and 22 other Ranks for Patrol duty. This patrol passed through the wire near BOAR COPSE about 10/45 p.m. on 1st July. 2/LIEUT. L.L. TYLER who was in charge of the patrol arrived at Battalion Headquarters Q.17 d.2.6 at about 1/15 a.m. on the 2nd July and reported that his patrol had been engaged with an enemy patrol about 30 or 40 strong and that 2/LIEUT. A. THORNALLAY and 10 other ranks were missing. As the relief of the Battalion had been carried the O/C 2/4 L.R. Lincoln Regt was asked to furnish a patrol for the purpose of searching for the missing officer and men. This Patrol was not ready and did not leave until about 2/30 A.M. The Patrol	

WAR DIARY

INTELLIGENCE SUMMARY

(Erase heading not required.)

Army Form C. 2118.

Page 2.

July 1917

Place	Date	Hour	Summary of Events and Information	Remarks and references to Appendices
			was taken charge of by 2/Lieut. R.E. GEE and 2/Lieut. L.L. TYLER (who was in charge of the first Patrol) accompanied it; they did not reach the wire until daylight and could not search the ground in front of our wire. The following are the casualties:- Killed - Officers nil; Other Ranks nil; Wounded - Officers nil; Other Ranks three; Missing - Officers nil; 2/Lieut A. THORNALLAY Other Ranks four.	
Equancourt 2nd		About 6 A.M. No. 202193 2/Cpl. B.D. Shaw "C" Coy and No 202090 Pte. H. Madeley "D" Coy, two Battalion Scouts volunteered to go back and search for the missing Officer and 11 men. They returned to the front line trench and went through our wire into "No Man's Land" in broad daylight. The ground is in full view of the enemy from several directions. They found one the missing: Killed - 2/Lieut A. THORNALLAY and 3 other ranks; Wounded - Officers nil; Other ranks one, Pte. Wilson R. No 202423 was severely wounded (GSW leg)	

WAR DIARY
INTELLIGENCE SUMMARY

July 1917 — Page 3

Army Form C. 2118.

Place	Date	Hour	Summary of Events and Information	Remarks and references to Appendices
Epéhy	6th		No. 202193 L/C. B.D. Shaw and No. 202070 Pte. H. Moseley carried him in. During this time they were frequently fired on. Their action undoubtedly prevented any identification being obtained by the enemy. One dead German soldier (31st R.I. Regt.) was also found which enabled the Regiment of the enemy on that Sector to be identified. For the above the Company Commander has awarded L/C. B.D. Shaw and Pte. H. Moseley, the Military Medal.	
			2/Lieut J.F. BOURNE attached to 2/6th. South Staffs Regt as Transport Officer.	
Barastre	7th		The Battalion proceeded by March Route to BARASTRE. Reference Sheet 57c S.W. O.10 c.o.3.	
	9th		Lieut. Col. J.A. ARMSTRONG proceeded to Hospital. Lieut-Col. J.H. POTTER, 2/6th North Staffs Regt, was posted to the Battalion and took over command on that date.	
	16th		Major A.C. BOOTH, 1/10th Manchester Regt, rejoined his Regiment.	

WAR DIARY
or
INTELLIGENCE SUMMARY.
(Erase heading not required.)

Army Form C. 2118.

July 1917. Page 4.

Place	Date	Hour	Summary of Events and Information	Remarks and references to Appendices
Bienvillers	16th		Major J.H. Thursfield M.C. 2/6th South Staffs Regt. posted to the Battalion and took over the duties of 2nd in Command.	GG
	20th		L/c B.D. Shaw & Pte. H. Madeley were presented with ribbons of Military Medal on parade by Brig. Gen. R.A. Currie D.S.O. Commdg. 176th Infantry Brigade.	GG

L.H. Porter
Lieut.-Col.
Commanding 2/5th South Staffs. Regt.

WAR DIARY

~~INTELLIGENCE SUMMARY~~
(Erase heading not required.)

Army Form C. 2118.

Vol 7
Confidential
17/59
S.7

Original

War Diary
of
2/5th Bn. South Staffordshire Regiment

From: 1st August 1917
To: 31st August 1917.

WAR DIARY or INTELLIGENCE SUMMARY

Army Form C. 2118.

Page 5 Vol II

August 1917

Place	Date	Hour	Summary of Events and Information	Remarks and references to Appendices
BARASTRE	24"		The battalion moved by motor bus and route march from BARASTRE	App I Page 1
		6	BOUZINCOURT	
		8-30	Departed by motor bus from BARASTE	
		11-30	Arrived at road junction 1 mile S.W of LE SARS Ref Map 57d and M.26.b.2.8	
		13-0	Departed from LE SARS by route march	
		16-15	Arrived at BOUZINCOURT V.13.a.9.9 where the battalion was billeted in the village	QQ
BOUZINCOURT	31st		The battalion moved by motor bus route and rail from BOUZINCOURT	App II Page IV
		6	WINNEZEELE via ABEELE and STEENVOORDE	
		3-20	Departed from BOUZINCOURT by route march	
		4-11	Arrived at AVELUY Station	
		5-45	Departed by train from EVELUY	
		16-45	Arrived at HOPOUTRE about 1 mile S.W of POPERINGHE	
		19-0	Departed by march route from HOPOUTRE	
		23-15	Arrived at WINNEZEELE Map Ref Sheet 27 Belgium & France M.c.3.6 where the battalion went into camp.	QQ

J. H. Porter
LIEUT.-COL
COMMANDING 2/5TH SOUTH STAFFS. REGT.

SECRET   2/5th Bn. South Staffordshire Regiment.   Copy No.......

Operation Orders No.30.

Ref.Map. 57 c & d. Scale 1/40,000.
Albert combined sheet 1/40,000.   22nd. August/17.

Appendix 1.
Page 1

1. **MOVE.**
The Battalion will move by Motor Bus and March Route tomorrow 23rd instant to BOUZINCOURT.

2. **STARTING POINT.**
The starting point will be Crucifix corner O.15 b.95.70.

3. **TIME OF PARADE.**
The Battalion will parade at 8-0 a.m. The head of the Column will be at the starting point at 8-30 a.m. The Battalion will be in groups of 25 men every 10 yards off the road on the Right or West Side of the Road, ready to embus.

4. **ORDER OF MARCH.**
Headquarters, Drums, A, B, C, & D Companies.

5. **HALFWAY RENDEZVOUS.**
The half way rendezvous will be at the road junction 1 mile S.W. of LE SARS M.26.b.2.8. On arrival at the half way rendezvous the Battalion will debus and will remain in their groups of 25, between the bus and the Right Side of the road, until the whole of the busses have passed. Further Orders will then be issued.

6. **TRANSPORT.**
The First Line Transport plus Baggage wagons will be Brigaded and will be under the Orders of the Brigade Transport Officer. They will proceed by Road and will be at the starting point O.15 a.1.5. at 6 a.m. Route Crucifix Corner O.8.a.1.4.-O.7.c .9.3. -
REINCOURT -LES BAPAUME - Main road to Bapaume.
Main Albert Road, thence Through ALBERT. All limbers will be fully loaded in accordance with Mob. Store Table.

7. **INTERVALS ON MARCH.**   etc.
Intervals between Battalions and Companies will be as follows:-
From Starting point 500 Yards between each group of 20 busses.
100 Yards between Companies From Debussing point to X.9.c.8.8.
500 Yards between Battalions and 200 yards between Companies.
after which 100 yards will be maintained between Companies.

                                                          (Sd). G. GARRETT.
Distribution:- Copy No.1. C.O.   Captain and Adjutant.
                    2. File.
                    3. Adjutant.
                    4. O.C. "A" Company.
                    5. O.C. "B"   "
                    6. O.C. "C"   "
                    7. O.C. "D"   "

2/5th BN. SOUTH STAFFORDSHIRE REGIMENT.
Instructions No. 1. issued in conjunction with
Operation Orders No. 30. dated 22/8/17.

Page 2

1. DRESS.
The Battalion will parade at 8 a.m. Dress Marching Order. for all ranks. Sandbags will not be carried.. Mounted Officers will not wear packs, these will be placed in their Company Limbers.. All Mounts will be in Marching Order, Officers Macintoshes rolled in rear of the Saddle.

2. BREAKFAST.
Breakfast will be at 4-30 a.m. Haversack rations will be carried by each man. All water bottles will be filled and willnot be used except under orders of the Commanding Officer.

3. HEAVY BAGGAGE.
All heavy Baggage will be stacked near the Quartermasters Stores ready for loading by 8 p.m. tonight, and will be loaded at 5-15 a.m. tomorrow 23rd instant.

4. OFFICERS KITS.
All Officers kits will be stacked near the Quartermasters Stores ready for loading at 4-45 a.m.

5. TRANSPORT.
All Transport will be loaded and ready to leave Camp at 5-30 a.m. Limbers will be loaded tonight. The Company Cookers and Officers Mess Cart must be ready to move at this hour.

6. OFFICERS MOUNTS.
All Officers Grooms with the Officers Mounts will leave Camp with the Transport, halting at debussing point at the half way rendezvous at M.26.b.2.8. (1 Mile S.W. of LE SARS). where they will await the arrival of the Battalion. Horses must be kept clear of the road at this point, so as not to interfere with traffic.

7. COMPANY LINES AND TENTS.
O's C. Companies will be held responsible that the whole of their Company lines are scrupulously clean. That all Tent flies are properly rolled up and that their Company Cook houses and Latrines are also clean. The N.C.O. i/c Pioneers, Shoemakers and Tailors are responsible that their shops are left properly clean. Officers Servants will be responsible for the cleaning of the Officers Lines and the P.M.C. will detail an Officer to see that the Officers Mess Kitchen and Cookhouse is perfectly before the Battalion moves. On no account is any existing structures to be removed or damaged. All ranks will be clear of the Camp at 7-30 a.m.

8. BAGGAGE WAGGONS.
Baggage wagons will report this evening and will proceed with 1st Line Transport at 5-30 a.m. tomorrow 23rd instant. They will rejoin No. 2 Company of the Train on completion of the march. A Loading Party 1 Sgt and 10 Other Ranks will be detailed by the Regimental Sergt. Major to load these wagons.

9. MOTOR LORRY.
One Motor lorry has been alloted to the battalion and will be at Bde. H.Qrs. at 5 a.m. 23rd inst. A Guide will be detailed by R.S.M. to bring the Lorry along road to Quartermasters Stores A Loading Party of 1 Sergeant and 12 other ranks will be detailed by R.S.M. to load the heavy Baggage. The A/Qmr. and 2 men will travel on this Lorry.

10. SURPLUS STORES AND BAGGAGE.
All Surplus Stores and Baggage, including any Blankets not taken by Units will be dumped at ROCQUIGNY station in accordance with Divisional Administrative Instruction No. 6 para. 4. It will be some time before any Stores so dumped are delivered to Units again.

11. RE. and Training Material.
All R.E. and Training Stores not taken with Units will be dumped in the course of tomorrow at Brigade Headquarters.

12. **SUPPLIES.**

The supply of Rations for Consumption on the 23rd. and 24th insts. will be as laid down in para. 3 of 59th. Divisional Instructions No. 6.

Refilling point from the 24th. inst. inclusive will be on the Main Road to between BOUZINCOURT and HEDAUVILLE immediately outside BOUZINCOURT.

Units will draw with 1st. Line Transport unless otherwise advised

13. **ORDNANCE STORES.**

No further issue of Ordnance Stores will be made until completion of move.

14. **POSTAL ARRANGEMENTS.**

No letters will be taken in at the Brigade Post Office on the 23rd. inst. On completion of move the Post Office will be located at BOUZINCOURT with No. 2 Coy. of the Train.

22..8..1917.

(Signed) GEO. GARRETT.
-Captain and Adjutant.

SECRET.   2/5TH. BN. SOUTH STAFFORDSHIRE REGIMENT.   Copy No. 3

ADMINISTRATIVE INSTRUCTIONS No. 1.

Appendix II
Page 1

Move of Division by strategical trains.

MOVE.

The Battalion will move by strategical Trains on or about 30th instant. Attention is Directed to Battalion Circular No. 1.

ENTRAINING STATION.

The entraining Station for the Battalion will be AVELUY.

MARCH.

The march to the entraining station will be carried out in accordance with the march table, to be issued later. Lieut. W.T. Butler is to reconnoitre this road at once. In the case of the 176th and 178th Infantry Brigades this road reconnaisance is to be compared by the two Brigades so that orders may be issued to avoid congestion on the road between BOUZINCOURT AND AVELUY.

TIME.

Railway time-tables will be issued on the evening of 28h inst. Trains leave the station at 4 hour intervals, e.g. (times imaginary).
AVELUY.
1. p.m.
5. p.m.

TRANSPORT.

Baggage and Supply Wagons will be issued to units before the March and and will accompany Units on the Train fully loaded. They will rejoin Train Companies after arrival at destination.

ACCOMMODATION

Each Train accommodated 1 Battalion less 1 Company. The odd Company of the first Battalion which entrains provides two working parties of 125 O.R. each. One party goes in the first train with Brigade Headquarters and unloads for the whole Brigade Group at the detrainment station. The other party loads for the whole Brigade Group at the entrainment Station and travels in the last train. This latter party must report to the R.T.O. 3½ hours before train departure time.

ADVANCE PARTIES.

Advance parties of 1 Officer per Unit and one N.C.O. per Company etc., will leave by train on 28th inst at a time to be communicated later.

SUPPLIES.

Rations and forage for Units departing from entraining Stations before 7 p.m. on 30th inst will be carried as follows:-
For consumption 30th instant. - on the men.
" "   31st "   - In Supply wagons on the Train.
" "   1st September - in 59 D.S.C. (proceeding by road).
and for Units departing from entraining Stations at or after 7 p.m. 30th inst. as follows:-
For consumption 31st inst. - on the men.
" "   1st Sept. - in Supply Wagons on the Train.

(Sd). G. GARRETT.
Captain and Adjutant.
2/5th South Staffordshire Regiment.

27/8/17.

Distribution:- Copy No.1. C.O.
2. 2nd in Command.
3. Adjutant.
4. O.C. "A" Coy.
5. O.C. "B" "
6. O.C. "C" "
7. O.C. "D" "
No 8. Lt. BUTLER.
9. Trans. Offr.
10. Quartermaster.
11. File

SECRET. 2/5TH. BN. SOUTH STAFFORDSHIRE REGIMENT.

BATTALION CIRCULAR No. 1.

ENTRAINMENT BY STRATEGICAL TRAINS.

The following General Instructions as to entrainment by strategical trains are issued for guidance:-

1. Entraining Stations will be notified later.

2. (a) All Trains consist of 1 Officers' Carriage: 17 Flat trucks: 30 Covered Trucks.
   (b) Each flat truck will take an average of Four Axles.
   Each covered truck will take 40 men, or 6 H.D. Horses or 8 L.D horses or Mules.
   (c) No personnel or stores will be allowed in the brake vans at each end of the train, or on the roofs of the Trucks. No covered Truck should be used for Baggage, as it restricts the space available for personnel.

3. Orders for the Battalion:- The Transport will arrive at the entraining station three hours before the time of the departure of the train, and the personnel one and a half hours.

4. A complete marching out state showing the number of men, horses, G.S. limbered G.S. and 2 Wheeled Wagons, and bicycles, should be sent down with the Transport of each Unit, so that the accommodation on the Train can be checked by the R.T.O. at the beginning of the entrainment, limbered G.S. Wagons being counted as two 2 Wheeled vehicles on the state.

5. Supply and Baggage Wagons will accompany the Battalion.

6. The entrainment of the Battalion must be completed half an hour before the time of departure of the Train, when it will be moved from the loading siding.

7. Breast Ropes for Horse Trucks will be provided by the Battalion, ropes for lashing vehicles on the flat trucks will be provided by the Railway.

8. Picquets must be provided at all stops for each end of the train to prevent troops leaving.

(Sd) G. GARRETT.
Captain and Adjutant.
2/5th South Staffordshire Regiment.

27/8/17.

SECRET.   Copy No... 3.

2/5th. BN. SOUTH STAFFORDSHIRE REGIMENT.
ADMINISTRATIVE INSTRUCTIONS No. 2.
Move of Division by Strategical Trains.

Page III

1. The following instructions are given in continuation of Administrative Instructions No.1.

2. **WORKING PARTIES.**
   Substitute the following for the instructions contained under the heading "accommodation" of Admin. Ins. No. 1:—
   Loading and unloading Working Party will be furnished as follows:—
   D Company under the Command of CAPT. R.M. CRAIG with cooker and team will Travel complete on the Brigade Headquarters Train to detraining Station. It will report to the R.T.O. there and be responsible for the unloading of all trains of the Brigade Group. 1 Company of the 2/6th North Staffordshire Regiment will report to the R.T.O. at the entraining station 3½ hours before the departure time of the first train, and will be responsible for the loading of all Trains of the Brigade Group. It will itself entrain on the last Train.

3. **BAGGAGE.**
   All Baggage and Equipment surplus to the loads of Vehicles is to be ready by 10 a.m. on the 29th inst, and will be dumped in the entraining Station Yard on sites to be pointed out by the R.T.O. concerned: it will then be man-handled on to the Train containing the Units to which it belongs and loaded under the Vehicles on the flats. Not more than 8 Lorry Loads per Brigade Group can be carried on the Trains, or dumped in the Station Yard. Lorries will be detailed to report to Brigade Headquarters on the 29th instant, and accommodation on them is to be allotted to all Units of the Brigade Group.
   The Quartermaster will arrange for Rations to be sent with a Guard of 2 men who will be detailed to look after the Kits at the Station.
   No extra Transport will be available above the Two Baggage Wagons for moving Stores and Kits on the 30th instant.

4. **DRESS.**
   All ranks will march to the Station and entrain in Marching Order.

5. **COMPOSITION OF TRAINS.**   Station: AVELUY.

Train. No.	Serial No.	Unit.	Division's Remarks.
	21.a.	D Company. 1 Cooker & Team of "A" Battalion.	5th South Stafford. Regt.
	21.	"A" Battalion (less 21.a.)	5th South Staffs. Regt.

(Sd). GEO. GARRETT.
Captain and Adjutant.
2/5th South Staffordshire Regt.

Distribution:— Copy No. 1. C.O.
2. 2nd in Command.
3. Adjutant.
4. O.C. "A" Coy.
5. O.C. "B" "
6. O.C. "C" "
7. O.C. "D" "
8. Lt. W.T. BUTLER.
9. Transport Officer.
10. Quartermaster.
11. File.

29/8/17

Page IV

2/5th. South Stafford Regiment.

MARCHE ENTRAIN TABLE

Entraining Station:- AVELUY.

Train No.	Serial No.	Unit	Starting Point	Time	Route	Due at Station	Remarks
2	21a	1 Cooker 5th. S.S.	W 14 b 2	9. 10/40 p.m. 29/8.	Via W 16 b 7 4.	11/11 p.m.	Transport only
2	21a	"D" Coy. 5th. S.S.	do.	11/55 p.m. 29/8	do.	12/41 a.m. 30/8	Less Transport
5	21	2/5 S.S. less 21a	do.	2/15 a.m. 30/8	do.	2/46 a.m. 30/8	Transport only
5	21	2/5th. S.S.R.	do.	3/35 a.m. 30/8	do.	4/16 a.m. 30/8	Less Transport.

Sick 9.30 a.m.

28/8/17

SECRET.　　2/5TH. BN. SOUTH STAFFORDSHIRE REGIMENT.　　Copy No...1...

OPERATION ORDER No. 33.

Page V

Ref. Map. Sheet 57 D 1/40,000.
and ALBERT Combined Sheet.　　　　　　　　　　　29th August/17.

1. The Battalion will entrain on August 30th at AVELUY Station in accordance with the undermentioned Time Table.

2. The Battalion less "D" Company will parade in sufficient time to pass Church Bouzincourt at 3-20 a.m. 30th inst. "D" Company will parade in sufficient time to pass Church BOUZINCOURT at 11-40 p.m. 29th instant.

3. The Train leaves 3 hours after the Transport and 1½ hours after the Infantry and dismounted details, are timed to arrive at the Station.

4. Transport and Troops marching to the Trains will not halt on the roads outside the station, but are to assemble in the forming up places as soon as possible. Transport will enter the Station yard only by the entrance nearest AVELUY village and troops only by the second entrance from the village. Wagons are to be drawn up as near to the Loading Lamps as possible, and horses then unhooked and taken to water before entraining

5. ROUTE:- BOUZINCOURT - Aveluy Road.

6. Starting point ⎫
　　　　　　　　　　⎬ See Time Table.
7. TIME　　　　　　⎭

8. Dress for all ranks:- Full Marching Order.

Signallers.
Headquarters.
Drummers.
"A" Company.
"B"　　"
"C"　　"

9. Order of march as per margin.

10. Transport:- "D" Company Cooker will leave the Church BOUZINCOURT at 10-25 p.m. 29th August 1917. complete, this which is proceeding with the Brigade Headquarters. The remainder of the Transport and Officers Mounts will parade under the Transport Officer in sufficient time to leave the Church BOUZINCOURT at 2 a.m. 30th August 1917.

11. All ranks must be warned that on no account are they to leave the Train unless they have orders to do so. Officer Commanding the Company in Front of the Train and the Officer Commanding the Company in the rear of the Train will detail Picquets in accordance with Battalion Circular No. 1 dated 27/8/17 para 8.

12. Water Bottles. All Water Bottles will be filled with tea.

13. Intervals. After leaving detraining station 500 yards interval will be maintained between Unit and Transport.

P.T.O.

Geo Garrett Capt Adjt
2/5 Staffs Regt

DISTRIBUTION:-

Copy No. 1 C.O.
2 2nd. in Command
3 Adjutant
4 O.C. "A" Company
5 O.C. "B" Company
6 PO.C. "C" Company
7 O.C. "D" Company
8 O.C. Headquarters (Lt. Butler)
9 Transport Officer
10 Medical Officer
11 Quartermaster
12 File

Army Form C. 2118.

WAR DIARY
or
INTELLIGENCE SUMMARY.
(Erase heading not required.)

Vol 8

Confidential

Original

War Diary
of
2/5th Bn. South Stafford Regiment

From:- 1st Sept 1917
To:- 30th Sept 1917

WAR DIARY or INTELLIGENCE SUMMARY.

Army Form C. 2118.

Volume II Page 6

September 1917.

Place	Date	Hour	Summary of Events and Information	Remarks and references to Appendices
WINNEZEELE	1	4.0	Strength of Battalion 35 Officers 1082 O.R.	
do	19	10.30	The Battalion moved by march and Bus Route to BRANDHOEK map reference Sheet 28 NW H.1.t.8.9	G.S.
BRANDHOEK		15.45	The Battalion arrived and encamped at RED ROSE CAMP	
do	21	16.10	The Battalion moved by march Route to GOLDFISH CHATEAU, YPRES NORTH AREA Map reference Sheet 28 NW H.11.L.1.1. Quartermaster Stores, Details and rear Battalion Headquarters remained at RED ROSE CAMP under Major J.H. Thursfield	G.S.
GOLDFISH CHATEAU		17.0	The Battalion arrived and encamped.	
do	22	15.30	Orders received that the Battalion would relieve the supporting Battalion of the Right Brigade of the 55th Division EAST of WIELTJE 'B' Company on the GALLIPOLI and 'A' Coy on LENS and IBERIAN and 'C' and 'D' companies on the CAMBRAI Switch Reserve line 300 yards EAST of WIELTJE. Dug in.	
do		17.30	The Battalion left GOLDFISH CHATEAU and marched through YPRES - ST. JEAN - WIELTJE and took up the above dispositions, relieving Battalions of the 55th Division which had become much cut up owing to heavy casualties. Battalion	

N.F. Porter, LIEUT.-COL.
COMMANDING 2/5TH SOUTH STAFFS. REGT.

WAR DIARY
or
INTELLIGENCE SUMMARY.

Volume II Page 7

September 1917

Army Form C. 2118.

(Erase heading not required.)

Place	Date	Hour	Summary of Events and Information	Remarks and references to Appendices
BANK FARM	23		Headquarters established at BANK FARM. Map reference Frezenburg Sheet C 24 b 3.6.	QL
		6.0	Very heavy enemy barrage on HILL 35 - LENS and BANK FARM.	
		13.0	Very heavy enemy barrage put down on front line occupied by 2/6th South Stafford Regt and on this line GALLIPOLI - LENS and IBERIAN. Enemy counter attack developed against HILL 37. "B" Coy moved forward from GALLIPOLI to support "A" Coy 2/6 South Staffs Regt on HILL 37. "C" Coy moved forward to reinforce GALLIPOLI and "D" Company was moved forward and dug a line of Trench Boyards WEST of the Brook of HILL 35. Casualties K. 1 W.O. Officer 5 OR - W 1 W.O. Officer 13 OR - M 1 W.O. Officer 116 OR.	QL
	24	6.0	"B" Coy withdrew to GALLIPOLI when everything was quiet.	
		22.30	The Battalion was relieved by the 2/4th and 2/5th LEICESTER Regts and 2/6th SHERWOOD FORESTER Regiments as follows:- "A" Coy by the 2/4th Leicester Regiment. "B" & "C" Coys by the 2/6th Sherwood Forester Regiment. "D" Coy by the 2/5th Leicester Regiment.	

L.H. Parker LIEUT.-COL.
COMMANDING 2/5TH SOUTH STAFFS. REGT.

WAR DIARY or INTELLIGENCE SUMMARY

Army Form C. 2118.

September 1917. Volume II Page 8.

Place	Date	Hour	Summary of Events and Information	Remarks and references to Appendices
			The relief was completed by 12 midnight and the Battalion marched back to GOLDFISH CHATEAU. Casualties K. this Officers 1 OR. – W. 10ff. 13 OR – M. this Officers 1 OR. 2/Lieut. E.C. NURSE wounded.	99
GOLDFISH CHATEAU	25	3.0	The Battalion arrived and Headquarters established.	
		23.30	The Battalion moved to take up position EAST of POMMERN CASTLE in support of the attack of the 177th Brigade which was to take place at dawn the following morning. Battalion Headquarters at POMMERN CASTLE that reference Sheet Inzenweg D.19.a.3.2.	99 23
POMMERN CASTLE	26	3.0	The Battalion carried on position and dug in preparatory to the attack.	
		5.50	Zero hour for 59th Divisional attack. The Battalion advanced in support to the 177th Brigade attack. 'A' and 'D' Coys in front line 'C' Coy nothing and 'B' Coy bringing up. The Battalion passed through 2/4th LEICESTER Regiment who had taken the first objective and aided the 2/4th LINCOLN Regt. in gaining the 2nd objective. After the capture of the final objective the Battalion dug itself in on a line running N.E. from PRIMROSE COTTAGES map	

W. J. Foster Lieut.-Col.
COMMANDING 2/5TH SOUTH STAFFS. REGT.

WAR DIARY
or
INTELLIGENCE SUMMARY. Volume II Page 9

(Erase heading not required.)

Army Form C. 2118.

September 1917

Place	Date	Hour	Summary of Events and Information	Remarks and references to Appendices
SHELL HOLE EAST OF PRIMROSE COTTAGE	26	18.0	Reference Sheet 28 NE. D.20.b.30.65 to D.20.b.85.45 in support to the 2/4th LINCOLN Regt. All objectives of the 59th Division gained. 15 prisoners and 1 machine gun captured by this Battalion during the course of the operations.	
		19.0	Very heavy enemy Barrage put down over the whole of the captured ground.	
			Enemy counter attack and 2 battalions moved forward in support of the 2/4th LINCOLN Regiment. The counter attack was broken up by our guns and machine gun fire into this supporting Battalion. Companies withdrew to shell holes 30 yds South of Headquarters were established in a shell hole 30 yds South of PRIMROSE COTTAGE. Casualties K. 1 Officer 30 OR — W. 8 Officers 7th OR — M. NC Officers 8 OR. Officers killed Capt. C.V.T. HAWKINS. — Wounded - 2/Lieuts. S.A. EGLINGTON; J.H. CROWE; H.V. CROOKE Capt. A.W. BROWN	
	27	21.0	Very heavy enemy shelling continued during the day. Heavy enemy barrage from 18.00 19.45. Battalion withdrew to CAMBRAI Reserve Trench EAST OF WIELTJE map.	

J.H. [signature]
LIEUT.-COL
COMMANDING 2/5TH SOUTH STAFFS. REGT.

WAR DIARY or INTELLIGENCE SUMMARY

Army Form C. 2118.
Volume II Page 10

September 1917

Place	Date	Hour	Summary of Events and Information	Remarks and references to Appendices
	1 September 1917		reference Sheet 28 NW. C.23 Central. Battalion Headquarters established in Dug Out at JUNCTION CAMBRAI Reserve Trench and WIELTJE - GRAVENSTAFEL Road. Casualties K rile Officers 15 O.R. W. 2 Officers 33 OR. M. hill Officers H.O.R. Officers Wounded 2/Lieut. G.E. STANLEY and Thayer J.H. THURSFIELD (at duty)	O.G
WIELTJE Dugouts	28	22.0	The Battalion was relieved by the CANTERBURY Battalion NEW ZEALAND INFANTRY and on relief proceeded by March Route through ST JEAN and YPRES to VLAMERTINGHE in Barns. Main reference Sheet 28 NW H.9.a.5.1. Carrying parties were found for the 177th Brigade. Casualties W. 1 Offr. 5 Ohr Thr 2/Lt E.T MELVILLE	O.G
	29	4.30	The Battalion arrived at VLAMERTINGHE Infantry Camp.	O.G.
VLAMERTINGHE		16.0	The Battalion moved by Bus Route to WATOU No.3 Area and went into Camp. Map reference Sheet 27 K.5 c 65.30	O.G
WATOU	30		The Battalion rested and refit and spent the day in cleaning up after coming out of action	O.G

F.H Porter
LIEUT.-COL.
COMMANDING 2/5TH SOUTH STAFFS REGT

SECRET.

2/5th Bn. SOUTH STAFFORDSHIRE REGIMENT.   Copy No... 3......

ADMINISTRATIVE INSTRUCTIONS NO. 3.

Move of Division by strategical trains.

Page VI

POSTPONEMENT.

Reference Administrative Instructions No. 2. dated 28/8/17.

The Move has been postponed for 24 hours.

Orders and Times will remain the same.

(sd). G. GARRETT.
Captain and Adjutant.

29/8/17.

Army Form C. 2118.

WAR DIARY
or
INTELLIGENCE SUMMARY
(Erase heading not required.)

Vol 9

Original

2/5th South Staffs. Regiment

War Diary
of

From: 1st Oct 1917
To:- 31st Oct 1917

Confidential

S.9

WAR DIARY
or
INTELLIGENCE SUMMARY.
(Erase heading not required.)

Army Form C. 2118.

October 1917   Vol II   Page 11

Place	Date	Hour	Summary of Events and Information	Remarks and references to Appendices
WATOU.	1st	6.0	Strength of Battalion 33 Officers 1081 O.Ranks.	
		6.30	The Battn. moved by Bus Route La GUARBECQUE and arrived at 4.30 p.m. by Road via STEENVORDE and HAZEBROUCK, arriving at 23.00	
GUARBECQUE	2nd		Inspection of the 176 Bde by Div. Commander when he expressed his thanks to all ranks for the recent success attained by the Division.	
	3rd	18.0	Orders received that the Battalion was to be prepared to move to ROMY AREA	
	4th	18.0	Orders received for 176 Infantry Brigade to move to ROMY AREA on 5th inst.	
	5th	1.0	Arrival of Draft of 4 offrs. 35 O.R. x Depot Bn. Most of these were Casuals from Hospitals	
		4.0	Arrival of Drafts of 9 men x Base Labours (5 Signallers & 4 Transport men)	

WAR DIARY or INTELLIGENCE SUMMARY

Army Form C. 2118.

October 1917. Vol II Page 12

Place	Date	Hour	Summary of Events and Information	Remarks and references to Appendices
GAURREQUE	4th	8.10	The Battalion less Transport moved by march and Bus Route to LISBOURG and arrived at 14.30. Transport moved by March Route and arrived at 15/30. Bgm estab at School in Village Square.	
LISBOURG	9th	16.0	Orders received that the Division would be prepared to move on 10th inst.	
	10th	2.30	Orders received that the Battalion would move by Bus Route to the GOUPIGNY Area on 10th inst.	
		6.30	The Battalion less Transport moved by Bus & march Route to SAINS-EN-GOHELLE arriving at debussing point HERSIN at 12/30 and proceeded by March Route to SAINS-EN-GOHELLE arriving at 15.00. The reconnaissance party of C.O., I.O. and Coy Comdrs proceeded by Bus and March Route from HERSIN to reconnoitre sector of Lille Held by 3rd Canadian Inf Bn who the Unit had been detailed to take over at an later date.	

WAR DIARY or INTELLIGENCE SUMMARY

Army Form C. 2118.

Vol II Page 13.

October 1919.

Place	Date	Hour	Summary of Events and Information	Remarks and references to Appendices
SAINS-EN-GOHELLE	10	8.30	The Transport proceeded by March Route to SAINS-EN-GOHELLE arriving at 23.00. Route PERNES – HARLIN – HERSIN – SAINS-EN-GOHELLE. B gr estab at H: 2. B. coy. (R.S.E.S.B.)	
SAINS-EN-GOHELLE	11	9.00	2nd i/c and 1 offr from each Coy proceeded to LEIVIN to reconnoitre position Rec'd by 1st Canadians & Battalion which this Bn: was to relieve on night of 12/13th inst.	
	12	15.0	Advance Party of 1 Officer & 4 Scouts Snipers & Runners proceeded to Front Line to take over Sniping Post etc.	
		17.30	The Battn paraded and proceeded by March Route to relieve 1st Canadian Infantry in Support Line at LEIVIN. Relief carried out without incident and completed by 21.00. B gr estab at M.23.c.2.3 Sheet LENS 36.c. S.W. 1/10000	

WAR DIARY
or
INTELLIGENCE SUMMARY

(Erase heading not required.)

Army Form C. 2118.

October 1914 V—II Page 14

Place	Date	Hour	Summary of Events and Information	Remarks and references to Appendices
LEIVIN	13th	10.0	Advance party of 1 Off and 1 NCO per Coy proceeded to front line trenches to take over French Stores etc from 1st Canadian Inf Bn	
		18.0	Relieved by 2/5th NSR and Battalion proceeded to relieve 2nd Bn 1st Bde 1st Canadian Divn in the Right Sector CITE-DE MOULIN Sheet 36 c S.W.1 1/10000 Hqrs estab at M 30-a-40-90 CITE-DE-RIAUMONT. Relief complete at 3/40 14th inst without incident	91
	14th	11.30	Enemy raided No 9 Post occupied by 1 NCO and 6 men of D Coy. Enemy repulsed by Bombs and Rifle fire. We had no casualties	91
		9.0	Transport moved from SAINS-EN-GOHELLE R 8.6 central to BOUVIGNY BOYEFFLES R.19.c. 86.50	
	15th	21.0	8 Officers reported for duty (6 gilted with 20 OR (Casuals))	
		18.0	Two Pls "D" Coy in Support relieved by B Coy on front line. A Coy relieving "D" Coy & "B" Coy Returning "C" Coy Relief completed at 1/30 16th Offrs OR	91
CITE DE RIAUMONT	16th		Casualties Killed Offrs OR Noel 1 3 Missing Pte 8 Pte 2/Lieut Jarvis	91

WAR DIARY
or
INTELLIGENCE SUMMARY.

(Erase heading not required.)

October 1917. Vol II Page 15

Army Form C. 2118.

Place	Date	Hour	Summary of Events and Information	Remarks and references to Appendices
CITE - DE RIAUMONT	17th/18th		Casualties NCOs & Men Adjd Offr. Nil OR 1 Missing NIL OR 1	
	18th/19th		" " " Nil OR 1	
	19th	18-0	The two Coys in Support relieved two Coys in front line "C" Coy relieving "A" Coy and "D" Coy relieving "B" Coy. Relief complete at 1/30 am. Casualties Nil	
	20th	5:10	Enemy heavy bombarded Front Line Coys with Trench Mortar &c. Our artillery was asked for Retaliation at 5.14 and Fire opened at 5.20 am the S.O.S. line.	
			At 5.17 am. the enemy attempted to raid No 18 & No 11. Posts of the Left Front Coy. Both raiding parties were driven off with Rifle fire and Bombs.	
		5.35	2nd attempt to raid No 11 Post and was driven off. A Platoon was moved forward nearer to the Front Line when the enemy Barrage opend so as to be ready for an immediate Counter attack	

WAR DIARY or INTELLIGENCE SUMMARY

Army Form C. 2118.

October 1914 / V III / Page 16

Place	Date	Hour	Summary of Events and Information	Remarks and references to Appendices
	20		The Platoon was not used and returned to its Post at Ecurie	
			Works. M 36 E. as soon as things quietened down.	
			Casualties Wounded 10 O.R.	QQ
	21	19.0	The Battalion was relieved by the 2/6 & SSR the right half	
			sec. of CITE-DE-MOULIN and on completion of relief proceded to	QQ
			CITE-DE-ROULLENCOURT as Battalion in Reserve. Relief completed	QQ
CITE-DE-			at 3 am. Casualties Nil.	QQ
ROULLENCOURT	22	5.0	Battalion Headquarters estab. at May. C 5.3.	
	23	11.30	Evening opened heavy shell fire and continued till 13/30	
		4.20	Shelling again resumed by enemy Casualties Killed 1 O.R. 2/Lieut	
			W.E. GODFREY Wounded 6 O.R. Lt Q.M. Sp. L.G. Harris reserved Army QQ	
	24		Major Keating took over Command of Bn. Vice Rifleet Potts on leave	QQ
	24	10.0	Enemy again shelled us heavily Casualties Killed 1 O.R. Wounded 2 O.R.	QQ
	28	9.0	Transport + Q.M. Stores moved from BOOVIGNY BOYEFFLES & CARENCY	QQ
	29		2/Lieut Grant reported for duty	QQ

WAR DIARY or INTELLIGENCE SUMMARY

Army Form C. 2118.

October 1914 Vol II Page 14

Place	Date	Hour	Summary of Events and Information	Remarks and references to Appendices
CITE - DE ROULLENCOURT.	29th		Q.M's Stores move completed. Casualties Rounded 2 O.R.	
		20.0	The Battalion was relieved by 2/4 Leicester Regt and proceeded by train from Red MLCC Siding May d.78 Es Vancouver	
	30th		Camp Chateau-de-la-Haye arriving at 23.0 2/Lts Nather and Meredith reported for duty.	

Markham
LIEUT.-COL.
COMMANDING 2/6TH SOUTH STAFFS. REGT.

Army Form C. 2118.

WAR DIARY
or
INTELLIGENCE SUMMARY.
(Erase heading not required.)

Vol 10

Original War Diary
of
2/5th Battn Staffs Regiment
from 1st Nov 1914
to 30th Nov 1914

Mini Brown (2)   S-10

Place	Date	Hour	Summary of Events and Information	Remarks and references to Appendices

Page 23

WAR DIARY
INTELLIGENCE SUMMARY.

Army Form C. 2118.

Place	Date	Hour	Summary of Events and Information	Remarks and references to Appendices
VANCOUVER CAMP.	1st Nov.	8.0	Strength Officers 37 Other Ranks 942	
CHATEAU-de-la-HAIE	"	14:30	The 176th Infantry Brigade formed and Military Medals and Divisional Cards were presented by MAJOR-GENERAL C.F. ROMER, C.B., C.M.G., A.D.C. commanding 59th Division to the following N.C.O's and men of the Battalion for acts of gallantry performed during the operations EAST of WIELTJE, between the 24th and 27th Sept. 1917.	
			No 201070. Sgt POULTON W. MILITARY MEDAL	
			No 201850. Dmr SHELDON C. MILITARY MEDAL	
			No 202109. Pte PEARSON H. MILITARY MEDAL	
			No 202791. Pte COLEMAN F. DIVISIONAL CARD	
			No 9746. Pte COWELL A. DIVISIONAL CARD	
			No 40760. Pte CROWTHER H. DIVISIONAL CARD	
			No 10123. Pte DIBBLE J. DIVISIONAL CARD	
			No 9172. LCpl DODD J. DIVISIONAL CARD	
			No 40468. Pte HAMMOND O. DIVISIONAL CARD	
			No 200337. LCpl HICKMAN L. DIVISIONAL CARD	
			No 201355. Pte PLANT D. DIVISIONAL CARD	
			No 202602. Pte VANNER F. DIVISIONAL CARD	
			No 201356. LCpl WOOD T. DIVISIONAL CARD	
VANCOUVER CAMP	5th Nov	19:30	A draft of three other ranks arrived from Base.	

J.J. Porter Lieut-Col.
COMMANDING 2/5TH SOUTH STAFFS REGT.

Page 24. II

Army Form C. 2118.

WAR DIARY
or
INTELLIGENCE SUMMARY.
(Erase heading not required.)

Instructions regarding War Diaries and Intelligence Summaries are contained in F. S. Regs., Part II. and the Staff Manual respectively. Title pages will be prepared in manuscript.

Place	Date	Hour	Summary of Events and Information	Remarks and references to Appendices
VANCOUVER CAMP	6/7	16:0	The Battalion entrained at SUMMIT SIDING Map Reference Sheet 36 B. and proceeded to RED TRENCH by train to relieve 2/7 SHERWOOD FORESTERS in the Right Sub Sector of the AVION SECTOR. The Battalion was disposed of as follows Two Coys in Front Line Trenches and two in Support. Battalion Headquarters had established at Map Reference Sheet QUEBEC ROAD T 2 b 20.80. Relief was completed by 2 oclock. Casualties Killed Offrs NIL. ORs NIL. - wounded Offrs NIL ORs NIL - missing Offrs NIL ORs NIL.	W.H.W.Q.2 GG
AVION SECTOR	8TH	5:0	Killed Offrs NIL ORs NIL - Wounded Offrs NIL ORs 1. Missing Offrs NIL ORs NIL.	GG
AVION SECTOR	9TH	17:0	Killed Offrs NIL ORs NIL - wounded Offrs NIL ORs 1 - missing Offrs NIL ORs NIL.	GG
AVION SECTOR	7TH 10/11	18:0	The two companies in Support relieved the two companies in the Front Line. Relief completed by 28 oclock. Battalion Headquarters moved to LA COULOTTE Map Reference Sheet VIMY 36° S.W. 3. N 31 C. 60.15. Battalion Head Qrs at T2 b 20.80 was occupied by one of the companies from Support Line.	GG
AVION SECTOR	11TH	12:30	Lt Colonel J.H. PORTER returned from leave and resumed command of the Battalion.	GG

J.H. Porter
COMMANDING 2/6TH SOUTH STAFFS. REGT.

Page 215
Army Form C. 2118.

WAR DIARY
or
INTELLIGENCE SUMMARY.
(Erase heading not required.)

Place	Date	Hour	Summary of Events and Information	Remarks and references to Appendices
AVION SECTOR	12TH	18:0	Major O.J.F. Hastings 2/6 NORTH STAFFS REGT. who was in command of the Battalion during its absence on leave of Lt Col. J.A. PORTER rejoined his unit on being relieved.	
		22:30	The enemy shelled A + C Companies positions with Gas Shells and Shrapnel. Casualties:- Killed Offrs Nil O.Rs Nil – Wounded Offrs Nil O.Rs Nil – Missing Offrs Nil O.Rs Nil.	
	13/14 7TH	18:0	The Battalion was relieved in the front line trenches RIGHT SUB-SECTOR, AVION SECTOR, by the 2/6 SOUTH STAFFS REGT. Relief was completed by 0/30 o'clock. On completion of relief the Battalion moved into support 3 Companies in RED TRENCH and 1 Company at GIVENCHY, Battalion Headqrs was established in RED TRENCH at map Reference Sheet VIMY 36c S.W.3. S.12.b.65.30.— Casualties:- Killed Offrs Nil O.Rs Nil Wounded Offrs Nil O.Rs Nil – Missing Offrs Nil O.Rs Nil. CAPT. W.H. CLAY M.C. 2/6 NORTH STAFFS REGT. posted to Battalion as 2nd in Command vice MAJOR J.H. THURSFIELD M.C. posted to DIVISIONAL REINFORCEMENT DEPOT.	
RED TRENCH.	15TH		LT. S.C. NOTT struck off strength of Battalion.	
	16/17 7TH	18:30	The Battalion was relieved by the 1/8 Battalion, CANADIAN INFANTRY BRIGADE in support line AVION SECTOR and proceeded by march route to ALBERTA CAMP SOUCHEZ arriving at 2:30 o'clock. Battalion Head Qrs situated at Refmap Sheet VIMY 36c SW.3. S.13.b.18.86. Casualties:- Killed Offrs Nil O.Rs Nil Wounded Offrs Nil O.Rs Nil Missing Offrs Nil O.Rs Nil	

Page 26IV
Army Form C. 2118.

WAR DIARY
or
INTELLIGENCE SUMMARY.
(Erase heading not required.)

Place	Date	Hour	Summary of Events and Information	Remarks and references to Appendices
ALBERTA CAMP SOUCHEZ. VIMY 36C S.W.3. S.13 & 18.86	17TH	14:30	The Battalion proceeded by march route to VANCOUVER CAMP. Reference sheet 36B. Battalion Head Qrs established at W.12 a 30.45.	GG
VANCOUVER CAMP CHATEAU-de-la-HAIE. SHEET 36 B. W.12 a 30.45	18TH	12:0	The Battalion proceeded by march route to GRAND SERVINS. Map Reference Sheet 36B. Head Qrs established at Q 34 b 5.7.	GG
GRAND SERVINS SHEET 36B. Q 34 b 5.7.	19TH	10:10	The Battalion less Transport proceeded by march route to BERNEVILLE. The Brigade halted at ACQ for mid-day meal, here at 12:30 o'clock, hereupon resumed at 15 o'clock arriving at BERNEVILLE 18:15 o'clock. Battalion Head Qrs were situated at 4 RUE-DE-WARLUS. Map Reference Sheet 51B Q 6 d 9.7.	GG
CARENCY	19TH	15:0	The Battalion 1st Line Transport proceeded by march route from CARENCY to BERNEVILLE to join Battalion arriving at BERNEVILLE at 20:0 o'clock.	GG
BERNEVILLE	19TH	21:0	Battalion ordered to be ready to move at half an hour's notice to COURCELLES-le-COMTE AREA.	GG
BERNEVILLE BERNEVILLE	20st 21	21:30 9:30 18:0	Battalion ordered to be ready to move by Bus, at one hour's notice to BAPAUME. Battalion Ordered to be ready to move at 1½ hour's notice to ACHIET-le-PETIT AREA. Draft of 20 O.Rs joined Battalion from Base.	GG
" "	"	20:21	Battalion ordered to proceed to COURCELLES-le-COMTE at once. The Battalion 1st Line Transport started with 1st Line Transport to COURCELLES-le-COMTE. The Battalion arrived at 3:30 o'clock on the 22nd. The march was greatly delayed owing to the route	W.A.

LIEUT. COL.
COMMANDING 2/5TH SOUTH STAFFS. REGT.

Page 27

Army Form C. 2118.

WAR DIARY
or
INTELLIGENCE SUMMARY.

(Erase heading not required.)

Place	Date	Hour	Summary of Events and Information	Remarks and references to Appendices
COURCELLES LE-COMTE.	23	14:0	Being blocked by other troops using the same route Battalion Head Qtrs were situated at Map Reference Sheet 57C A 16 c 85.90.	GC
			The Battalion less Transport proceeded by march route to ACHIET-le-GRAND where it entrained at 18:45 and proceeded to FINS where it detrained at 20:45 and proceeded by march route to RAILTON CAMP. HEUDECOURT arriving about 22:0 oclock. Battalion Head-245 Map Reference Sheet 57C Y.16.c.g.6.	
		15:0	The Battalion 1st Line Transport proceeded by road route to RAILTON CAMP HEUDECOURT arriving 2:30 oclock 24th inst.	GC
RAILTON CAMP.	27.	10:30	Battalion ordered to be ready to move at a moment's notice to BOURLON WOOD.	
"		12:0	Advance party proceeded to RIBECOURT.	
"		12:26	The Battalion accompanied by ECHELON "A" of 1st Line Transport, proceeded by march route to RIBECOURT arriving at 17:30 oclock	
			The Battalion on arriving at RIBECOURT relieved the 1st BATTN IRISH GUARDS who were in Reserve in the FONTAINE - NOTRE-DAME Sector. Batn Head Qtrs situated at Reference Map Sheet 57C L25 d 60.55. Echelon "B" 1st Line Transport proceeded to RIBECOURT by road route arriving 19:30 oclock.	GC
"		16:0		
RIBECOURT	27	23:30	Advance party 1 Offr per Coy. 1 N.C.O. per platoon, 2 runners per Coy and 2 runners from Batt. Head Qtrs, proceeded to Battalion Reflief Point	

COMMANDING 2/5TH SOUTH STAFFS. REGT.
LIEUT-COL.

Page 28

Army Form C. 2118.

WAR DIARY
or
INTELLIGENCE SUMMARY.
(Erase heading not required.)

Place	Date	Hour	Summary of Events and Information	Remarks and references to Appendices
RIBECOURT	28-29	16:45	At front line battalion FONTAINE-NOTRE-DAME SECTOR. To take over stores etc from 1st Batt'n SCOTS GUARDS. The battalion proceeded to front line trenches to relieve 1st Bn. SCOTS GUARDS in the FONTAINE-NOTRE-DAME SECTOR. The Battalion was disposed as follows 3 Companies in front line one Company in Support. Battalion Head-Dr^s situated at CANTAING MILL. Map Reference Sheet 57c F 26 a 7.5. Relief was completed by 21:45 o'clock. — Casualties — killed Offrs NIL ORs NIL wounded Offrs NIL ORs NIL missing offrs NIL ORs NIL.	
FONTAINE- NOTRE- DAME SECTOR.	29	19:30	Enemy shell 67° F 26 a 7.5. Brought up 3 ORs. Signallers joined Battalion from Base.	
"	30	8:15	The Enemy put down a very heavy barrage on the whole of the position occupied by the battalion. CANTAING MILL which was occupied by Batt^n Head-Dr^s was burnt down and ammunition dump destroyed. The enemy's barrage lasted from 8:15 o'clock till 15:30 o'clock. — Casualties — killed Offrs NIL ORs NIL wounded Offrs NIL ORs 24 missing Offrs NIL ORs 7.	

J.H. Porter
Lt Colonel
Commanding 2/6 South Staff^d Reg^t.

Army Form C. 2118.

WAR DIARY
or
INTELLIGENCE SUMMARY.

(Erase heading not required.)

Vol 11

Confidential

Original

War Diary
of
2/5th South Staffs Regiment.

From 1st Dec 1917
To 31st Dec 1917

S. 11

WAR DIARY
or
INTELLIGENCE SUMMARY.

Army Form C. 2118.

VOL. 11   Page 24.

(Erase heading not required.)

DECEMBER 1917.

Instructions regarding War Diaries and Intelligence Summaries are contained in F.S. Regs., Part II. and the Staff Manual respectively. Title pages will be prepared in manuscript.

Place	Date	Hour	Summary of Events and Information	Remarks and references to Appendices
FONTAINE NOTRE DAME SECTOR	1st.	6.0	Strength Officers 36 Other Ranks 819	
		13.0	The Enemy put down a very heavy barrage and made an attack on our right flank which was repulsed. An attack was next made on our left flank, the enemy being again repulsed. Battalion Headquarters was heavily shelled throughout the day all telephone wires being cut on several occasions.	A
		17.0	"D" Company which was in support near Battalion Headquarters was moved up to Front Line to reinforce it. One Company of the 2/5th. Battalion The Leicestershire Regiment was sent to the battalion as reinforcements and occupied the support trench which had been vacated by "D" Company. Casualties. X Officers nil, Other Ranks 7. Wounded-2/Lieut. G.S. Walker Other Ranks 10. Missing Officers nil, Other Ranks nil	A
	2nd.	5.30	Ration party heavily shelled. Casualties, Killed - Officers nil, Other Ranks 1. Wounded Officers nil, Other Ranks 3. Missing - Officers nil Other Ranks nil.	A
		19.0	On the night of the 2/3 December the battalion was relieved in the front line by the 2/5th Battalion The Leicestershire Regiment. The Enemy shelled Battalion Headquarters at CANTAING MILL P.25.d.7.5. and LA JUSTICE L.1.d.9.8. at intervals during the whole day.	A
	3rd.	0.30	Relief was completed at 0.30 o'clock on the 3rd. On completion of relief the battalion proceeded to the HINDENBURG Support Line south of FLESQUIERES. Battalion Headquarters were established at K.24.b.78.60. Ref. Map 57c 1/40,000 FRANCE. Casualties, Killed - Officers nil Other Ranks 1. Wounded - Officers nil, Other Ranks 3. Missing - Officers nil, Other Ranks nil.	A
		16.20	Orders received for one Company to be held in readiness to move at a moment's notice. Enemy were reported to be making an attack on MARCOING. Casualties - nil.	A
	4th.	12.0	Orders received that battalion would be relieved on the night of 4th/5th December. Advance Party left for new camp.	A
	5th	0.15	The Transport, which was at RIBECOURT proceeded under orders of the Brigade Transport Officer to the new camp. They halted for the night at HAVRINCOURT WOOD Ref. Map France 57c 1/40,000 P.18.c.4.3 and proceeded to GRAZING CAMP, LECHELLE at 15.30 o'clock arriving about 18.0 o'clock	A
		2.30	The battalion was relieved in the HINDENBURG Support line by the 2/4th. Battalion The Lincolnshire Regiment and on completion of the relief proceeded to HAVRINCOURT WOOD Ref. Map 57c France K.34.b.5.9 where it remained for the night	A

COMMANDING 2/5TH SOUTH STAFFS REGT.
LIEUT.-COL.

Army Form C. 2118.

WAR DIARY
INTELLIGENCE SUMMARY.

VOL. 11   Page 25.

(Erase heading not required.)

Instructions regarding War Diaries and Intelligence Summaries are contained in F.S. Regs., Part II. and the Staff Manual respectively. Title pages will be prepared in manuscript.

Place	Date	Hour	Summary of Events and Information	Remarks and references to Appendices
HAVRINCOURT WOOD	5th	10.15	The battalion left HAVRINCOURT WOOD and proceeded via METZ to camp in HAVRINCOURT WOOD Ref. Map France 57c 1/40,000 P.18.d.5.5 arriving about 14 o'clock	
		15.30	The battalion left the above camp and proceeded via NEUVILLE-YTRES to GRAZING CAMP, LECHELLE arriving about 17.30 o'clock. Battalion Headquarters was established at GRAZING CAMP Ref. Map France 57c.	
LECHELLE	6th	12.0	Orders received that the battalion was to be ready to move forward at one hours notice to support the 177th Infantry Brigade in the front line if the enemy attacked.	
	10th	13.30	The battalion left GRAZING CAMP, LECHELLE and proceeded to HINDENBURG Support Line to relieve the 2/7th Battalion The Sherwood Foresters. A halt was made in HAVRINCOURT WOOD Ref. Map 57c 1/40,000 P.18.d.5.5. The battalion left here at 16.45 o'clock and arrived at HINDENBURG Support Line, FLESQUIERES at 20.30 o'clock. Relief was completed about 23.0 o'clock. Battalion Headquarters was established at Map Ref. France 57c 1/40,000 K.24.d.4.4. During the relief the battalion was heavily shelled. Casualties. Killed Officers nil, Other Ranks 7. Wounded Capt. J.J.Atkinson, Other Ranks 15, Missing Officers nil, Other Ranks nil	
		14.0	Transport and Quartermaster's Stores proceeded to NEUVILLE Ref. Map 57c France P.22.d.3.5	
FLESQUIERES	12th	17.0	Enemy shelled position held by battalion for about 30 minutes. Casualties Killed Officers nil, Other Ranks 2. Wounded Officers nil Other Ranks 9. Missing Officers nil Other Ranks nil	
	13th	18.0	The battalion relieved the 2/6th. Battalion The Sherwood Foresters in the front line trenches Relief completed at 22.0 o'clock. The Battalion was distributed as follows:- Two Companies in the front line and two in support. Battalion Headquarters was established in FLESQUIERES Ref. Map 57c 1/40,000 K.18.c.17.35. Casualties - Killed Officers nil, Other Ranks nil. Wounded Officers nil Other Ranks 1. Missing Officers nil Other Ranks nil.	
	14th	8.0	Battalion Headquarters and village of FLESQUIERES was shelled throughout the day. Casualties Officers Killed Officers nil Other Ranks nil, Wounded Officers nil Other Ranks 1 Missing Officers nil Other Ranks nil	
	15th	8.0	Enemy aircraft active. Battalion Headquarters heavily shelled at intervals throughout the day. Casualties nil.	

LIEUT-Col.
COMMANDING 2/5TH SOUTH STAFFS.

WAR DIARY
or
INTELLIGENCE SUMMARY.

Army Form C. 2118.

Vol. 11   Page 25

Place	Date	Hour	Summary of Events and Information	Remarks and references to Appendices
OLD BRITISH FRONT LINE	16th	8.0 22.0	Battalion Headquarters shelled during day and night at intervals. Fighting Patrol from "D" Company under command of 2/Lt. W.J. Hand located enemy's position and captured a German prisoner belonging to the 104th. R.I.R. Casualties nil	
	17th	5.0 12.30	Enemy shelled Battalion Headquarters and village of ESNOULIERES at intervals during day and night. Transport and Quartermaster's Stores moved from NEUVILLE to MERLIMCOURT Ref. Map 57c 1/40,000 P.8.c.2.7	
	18th	8.0 18.0 23.0	Enemy shelled Battalion Headquarters and village during the day. On the night of the 18th/19th December the Battalion was relieved in the front line sector by the 5/6th. Battalion The Lincolnshire Regiment. Relief was completed by 21.0 o'clock. On completion of relief the battalion proceeded to the old British Front Line. Battalion Headquarters was established at Ref. Map France 57c 1522.c.7. Fighting patrol under the command of 2/Lt. D.C. Welsh surprised enemy working party and attacked them with bombs killing six and wounding others. One unwounded prisoner was taken. The remainder of the enemy fled.	
OLD BRITISH FRONT LINE	20th	14.0	The battalion was relieved by the 8th Battalion The South Staffordshire Regiment and on completion of relief proceeded to BARASTRE via NEUVILLE-LYNDE-BUS arriving in camp about 18.0 o'clock. Battalion Headquarters was established at Ref. Map France 57c 1/40,000 O.16.a.7.3	
BARASTRE	24th	5.30	Transport proceeded by march route via HAPLINCOURT-BANCOURT-BAPAUME-DILLCOURT-ACHIET-le-GRAND - ACHIET-le-PETIT to TINQUES.	
	25th	7.10	The battalion less transport proceeded by march and train route. Entraining at BAPAUME and detraining at TINQUES whence marched to MAIZE Ref. Map France 57c 1/40,000 arriving at 17.30 o'clock. Battalion Headquarters were established at DUCATEAU Chateau, MAIZE Ref. Map France 57c 1/40,000 I.18.b.2.3	

COMMANDING 2/5TH SOUTH STAFFS. REGT.

Army Form C. 2118.

WAR DIARY
or
INTELLIGENCE SUMMARY.
(Erase heading not required)

Instructions regarding War Diaries and Intelligence Summaries are contained in F.S. Regs., Part II. and the Staff Manual respectively. Title pages will be prepared in manuscript.

Confidential

Original

War Diary

of

2/5th Bn. South Staffs Regiment

From 1st Jan. 1918
to 31st Jan 1918

Army Form C. 2118.

WAR DIARY
or
INTELLIGENCE SUMMARY
(Erase heading not required.)

JANUARY 1918   Vol. II   Page 27

Place	Date	Hour	Summary of Events and Information	Remarks and references to Appendices
MARIN	Jan 1		**STRENGTH** Officers 35 Other Ranks 858	
			2/Lieut. C. C. Hedges, 4th Battalion The Royal Berkshire Regiment attached 2/5 Battalion The South Staffordshire Regiment awarded the "Military Cross".	
			2/Lieut. G. S. Walker, 2/5 Battalion The South Staffordshire Regiment awarded the "Military Cross"	
			Lieut.-Col. J. R. Porter, 2/5 Battalion The South Staffordshire Regiment awarded the "Distinguished Service Order" - New Year Honours Gazette	
	2	17.0	A draft of 10 Other Ranks arrived from Base	
	3	11.0		
	4	11.0	Captain J. S. Reid, The 2/5 Battalion South Staffordshire Regiment awarded the "Military Cross"	
			The Battalion was inspected by companies by BRIGADIER-GENERAL T.G.COPE D.S.O. commanding 176th Infantry Brigade. After the inspection the following Non-commissioned officers and men were presented with medals and cards by BRIGADIER-GENERAL T. G. COPE D.S.O.	
			202691 Sergt KIRTON F. - Distinguished Conduct Medal	
			200920 " HATTON S. - Military Medal	
			240130 Pte KEATINGS - Divisional Card	
			40750 " AUDY - Military Medal	
			32186 " ROBINSON - Military Medal	
			Division ordered to hold itself in readiness to move at 48 hours notice. Warning Order No. 1 issued to Companies.	
	5		No. 200021 Sergt GREGORY A. awarded the "Meritorious Service Medal" - New Year Honours Gazette	
			Major W. H. CLAY M.C. proceeded to England to attend 5th Senior Officers Course, ALDERSHOT and was struck off the strength of the battalion	
	11		Major R. S. PRATT M.C. 2/6 Battalion The Notts. and Derby. Regiment posted to this battalion as second-in-command vice Major W. H. CLAY.	
	16	12.0	Draft of 11 Officers arrived from Base	
	17	9.30	Battalion prepared for inspection by GENERAL HON. SIR J. H. G. BYNG K.C.B., K.C.M.G., M.V.O. commanding THIRD ARMY and MAJOR-GENERAL C. F. ROMER C.B., C.M.G., A.D.C. commanding 59th DIVISION but owing to the inclement weather the Inspection was cancelled	
	18	13.0	Draft of 35 Other Ranks arrived from Base	
	20	22.0	Information received that the 2/5 Battalion The South Staffordshire Regiment is to be disbanded	
	21	13.30	Advance party left for ACHIET-LE-GRAND	
	22	10.30	Main party, consisting of 3 Officers 146 Other Ranks, Lieut. Gladwin Capt. A. P. BUSWELL left for formation of Third Army Clearing Depot at ACHIET-LE-GRAND	
	24	1.00	Draft of 9 Other Ranks arrived from Base	
	26	14.30	Draft of 56 Other Ranks arrived from Base	

Army Form C. 2118.

WAR DIARY
or
INTELLIGENCE SUMMARY
(Erase heading not required.)

VOLUME 11   January 1918   Page 28

Instructions regarding War Diaries and Intelligence Summaries are contained in F.S. Regs., Part II. and the Staff Manual respectively. Title Pages will be prepared in manuscript.

Place	Date	Hour	Summary of Events and Information	Remarks and references to Appendices
ATH	27	10.00	Information received concerning the Units to which Officers and Other Ranks of this battalion are to be posted	35 in.
	28	18.00	Draft of 80 Other Ranks left to join 1/5 Batt. The South Staffordshire Regt.	35 in.
	28		Letter of regret and good wishes received from Field Marshall SIR DOUGLAS HAIG, K.T., G.C.B., G.C.V.O., K.C.I.E., Commander in Chief, British Armies in France	35 in.
	29	21.00	Main party of 3 Officers 148 Other Ranks returned from Third Army Clearing Depôt	35 in.
	30	11.00	Battalion paraded ready to march off to join new Units	
			The following parties entrained at FREVENT	
			1/5 Batt. The South Staffordshire Regt. — 4 Officers 116 Other Ranks	
			1/6 Batt. The South Staffordshire Regt. — 4 Officers 128 Other Ranks	
			2nd Batt. The South Staffordshire Regt. — 6 Officers 123 Other Ranks	
			4th Batt. The South Staffordshire Regt. — 3 Officers 85 Other Ranks	
			7th Batt. The South Staffordshire Regt. — 4 Officers 92 Other Ranks	
	31		Rear party of 1 Officer 25 Other Ranks returned from Third Army Clearing Depôt. ACHIET-LE-GRAND	35 in.
			Draft of 1 Officer and 23 Other Ranks entrained at FREVENT to join new Units	35 in.
			Battalion Headquarters staff and transport remained at DUCATEAU CHATEAU to wind up the affairs of the Battalion.	

Signed: J.H. Porter
Lieut. Col.
Commanding 2/5 Batt South Staffordshire Regt.

www.ingramcontent.com/pod-product-compliance
Lightning Source LLC
Chambersburg PA
CBHW081449160426
43193CB00013B/2416